A BOUQUET OF WORDS

Express Yourself through the Language of Flowers

MARY KELAVA

ILLUSTRATED BY CARRIE WASTERLAIN

A Bouquet of Words:
Express Yourself through the Language of Flowers

Copyright ©2023 Mary Kelava

Published by Mary Kelava, www.marykelava.com

All rights reserved. No part of this book may be reproduced or used in any manner without written permission of the copyright owner except for the use of quotations in a book review. For permission requests, contact Mary@marykelava.com

ISBN: 978-1-7380230-0-4 (Paperback)
ISBN: 978-1-7380230-2-8 (Hardcover)
ISBN: 978-1-7380230-1-1 (eBook)

Illustrations by Carrie Wasterlain, www.carrieandthebrush.com

Cover Layout and Interior Formatting by
Becky's Graphic Design®, LLC, www.beckysgraphicdesign.com

A BOUQUET OF WORDS

♡ Mary

Dedicated to my family

PINK TULIP

Caring

*There's rosemary, that's for remembrance.
Pray you, love, remember. and there
is pansies, that's for thoughts . . .*

WILLIAM SHAKESPEARE

PANSY

Thinking of you

TABLE OF CONTENTS

WELCOME

Welcome to A Bouquet of Words 3

I | CREATING MEANINGFUL MOMENTS

CREATING MEANINGFUL MOMENTS 9
- Gifts 10
- Gardens 15
- Events 18

II | YOUR GO-TO RESOURCES

YOUR GO-TO RESOURCES 27

Flower Catalogue 31
- Flowers 33
- Meanings 42

Specialty Lists 51
- Anniversary Years 52
- Birth Months 55
- Lunar New Year 58
- Zodiac 61
- The Significance of Colour 64
- 20 Flowers Readily Available All Year 65
- 15 of the Most Fragrant Flowers 67
- 12 Flowering Herbs 68
- 10 Popular Types of Greenery 69
- 10 Flowering Houseplants 70
- 10 Flowering Garden Plants 71
- 10 of the Easiest Flowers to Grow from Seed 72
- Flowers with More than one Common Name 73

Helpful Tips	75
Floral Lingo	76
Arrangement	77
Smooth Delivery	78
Be Kind to Our Environment	79
Budget	81
Flower Care	82

III | 'REMEMBER FOREVER' SPACE

Remember Forever Space	87
Calendars	99
Flower Gift Giving Dates	101
National Flower Dates	107
Personal Calendar	113

IV | AND THERE'S MORE

And There's More	121
Bonus Lists	122
Edible Flowers	123
Preserving Flowers	125
Flower Tourism	128
Floral Baby Names and Their Meanings	130
No Fresh Flowers—No Problem	131
Repurposing Flowers	134
About Me	143
Leave a Review	145

Welcome

WISTERIA

Welcome

MARY KELAVA

WELCOME TO A BOUQUET OF WORDS

IT'S WELL KNOWN THAT a red rose symbolises love, but what's not as well known is that all flowers have special meanings.

Flowers can express everything from *thank you* and *I'm thinking of you* to *welcome* and *good luck*. There are flowers with celebratory meanings and those that are more fitting for comfort during sorrowful times.

Using flowers to create and send messages is the language of flowers—or floriography.

A Bouquet of Words began with a seed of an idea after I read *The Language of Flowers*, a novel by Vanessa Diffenbaugh. Within the first few pages, I was captivated by the idea that each flower has its own meaning, and that just by your choice of flowers you can share your thoughts and sentiments with others.

This charming means of communication has been used for thousands of years and across all cultures, and yet in today's world it is relatively unknown. I wondered why. To me it sounded like such a fun, simple, and yet impactful way to express yourself.

It turns out there is a good reason why it is lacking in popularity. The language of flowers is not as straightforward as it first sounds. Every flower can have more than one meaning and sometimes those meanings are the total opposite of each other.

Let's look at the example of a sunflower: It can mean *adoration* because of the way it turns its face to the sun, or it can mean *haughtiness* because it can look like it's turning its nose up at something. You can see how this could be confusing.

I realised some changes needed to be made to make this language usable.

So while staying true to the roots of the language of flowers, I modernised and simplified it in three ways:

1. I scaled way back on the number of flowers a traditional book on this topic has. I kept my choices to only those flowers, herbs, and greenery that are most commonly known.

2. To eliminate long lists of meanings for each flower, I chose only one or two meanings that are relevant for today's world. You won't find any *forsaken*, *coquetry*, or *malevolence* in my book!

3. I focused only on positive meanings. Who needs flowers to say, *Thy frown will kill me*, *My best days are past*, or *I declare war against you?*

With these changes, rather than being overwhelmed by the language of flowers, you'll discover just how easy it is to choose the perfect flowers to share the exact sentiments you want.

If you are someone who gives flowers as gifts, plants flowers in your garden, or uses flowers at events, this book is for you. In it you will find the flower catalogue, which is your go-to guide of flowers and meanings, speciality lists for quick reference, helpful tips straight from a former florist (me), blank pages to make notes and keep records, calendars with special floral dates throughout the year, flower quotes, and floral memories.

Before you know it, you will be making your gifts more personalised, your events more memorable, and your gardens more meaningful.

A BOUQUET OF WORDS

FREESIA

Friendship/Ultimate trust

PART I

CREATING MEANINGFUL MOMENTS

A BOUQUET OF WORDS

Happiness is to hold flowers in both hands.

—JAPANESE PROVERB

CREATING MEANINGFUL MOMENTS

PART OF THE BEAUTY of the language of flowers is that it gives you an opportunity to reflect on the important people and moments in your life. Whether you use it to connect with others, or bring a sense of peace to yourself, it's a way to express your feelings with more than just words.

Let's look at how you can create meaningful moments through gifts, gardens, and events.

Gifts:

Give Flowers as Gifts — 10

Gardens:

Creating a Themed Garden — 15

Events:

Creating Meaningful Event Bouquets — 18

Gifts

Throughout history and across all cultures, flowers have been given as gifts. In fact, around the world they are one of the most popular gifts to give. If you wonder why this is so, consider the following:

- Flowers suit every occasion. I can't think of anything else versatile enough to say *happy birthday*, *congratulations*, *thank you*, *I'm sorry*, *get well soon*, or even just *I'm thinking of you*.
- Flowers are available in a wide price range to suit every budget.
- You can plan your gift of flowers in advance or arrange it on short notice.
- You can arrange for flower delivery anywhere in the world.
- Flowers are appropriate for someone you know well or someone you've never met before.
- The wide variety of flowers available means every floral gift can be unique.
- Flowers have been scientifically proven to lift people's spirits.

Now think about how incorporating the language of flowers into your floral gifts would give you the opportunity to make them even more special by not just *showing* someone how you feel but by also *telling* them.

What you may be surprised to discover is that creating messages with flowers is something that works equally well for someone you are close to, someone you haven't seen in a while, or someone you have just met.

For someone you are close to, choosing flowers based on your knowledge and memories of them will be a new way to express your sentiments. For someone you have lost touch with, sharing a bouquet with a meaningful message has the power to bring you back closer together. If you are giving a bouquet to someone you don't know well, it can be the beginning of a beautiful friendship.

When creating your bouquets, the key to being successful is to keep in mind two things: *who* you are giving the flowers to and *why* you are giving them.

When thinking about the 'who' you should consider what you know about the individual who will be receiving them. Looking at their character traits, things you admire about them, words that reflect your relationship, their favourite colour, and their favourite flower will all be helpful.

For the 'why', think about what sentiments best fit the occasion—joy, sorrow, best wishes, forgiveness, gratitude—and use the flowers that represent those emotions.

By focusing on these things, the bouquet you create using the language of flowers will be thoughtful and personalised.

Equally as important as creating your floral message is making sure the person receiving the flowers knows the meaning.

I find the best way to do this is to put it in writing. You could keep it as simple and straightforward as jotting down a list of the flowers you chose and their meanings, or you could craft a personalised language of flowers message—something special that may be kept for years to come.

Examples of a personalised message

A bouquet of pink tulips and chamomile for get-well wishes:

> *In the language of flowers, please know that I am thinking of you (pink tulips—caring) and I'm wishing you all the best as you work to regain your strength (chamomile—energy in adversity).*

An arrangement of ranunculus, yellow roses, and fern as a housewarming gift:

> *May warmth and beauty (ranunculus—radiant charm) fill your new home (fern—shelter) and bring you an abundance of joy (yellow rose—joy).*

A poinsettia plant as a Christmas gift:

> *Wishing you every happiness (poinsettia—good cheer) during this festive season.*

If you are using many different types of flowers, it may be too much to include each one and their meaning in the body of the text, so instead write something simple to convey the overall feeling and then follow with a list of the flowers and meanings (in this example I also include colours).

An arrangement for a new baby:

> *A sweet new baby to love and enjoy! Wishing you all the best as you begin this new phase in your life called parenthood.*

FLOWERS

Anemone—Anticipation

Baby's breath—Everlasting love

Daisy—Innocence

Carnation (pink)—Gratitude/Mother's love

Hyacinth (pink)—Playfulness

Eucalyptus—Protection

COLORS

White—Innocence/Purity

Pink (light)—Nurturing

Green (soft)—Freshness/Growth/Harmony

A BOUQUET of Words

ANEMONE

Anticipation

Gardens

My first floral memory is of sweet peas—fresh and fragrant, picked straight from the garden. When I was six years old we moved to the country. My mum planted a garden. It was mainly a vegetable garden, but at one end there was a trestle where sweet peas were planted. When they were ready we would go and pick the oh-so-fragrant blooms. To this day, every time I smell a sweet pea I think of that garden and those freshly picked sweet peas.

What I didn't know then (but do now) is that sweet peas hold the meanings of *blissful pleasures* and *thank you for a lovely time*. Both suit my memories well.

When I was older and heard about themed gardens, my mind went straight to the idea of creating one with the language of flowers.

If you're not familiar, any garden designed around a central idea is a themed garden. It could be one where all the flowers are the same colour, one that is a pollinating garden (flowers that specifically attract butterflies and bees), or one where all the flowers are edible. Whatever the concept, the point is that everything works together cohesively.

The key to a language of flowers garden is to pick a theme meaningful to you. Some suggestions are family, friends, joy, healing, remembrance, and relaxation. Choosing something that lets your creativity and personal experiences shine will make your garden a winner.

A BOUQUET OF WORDS

For ideas and inspiration that will support your chosen theme I recommend looking through the Flower Catalogue, as well as the Speciality Lists.

Here are a couple of examples to give you some ideas:

> *For the theme **family** you could plant the birth month flower for each family member, plant a flower with a meaning you think represents each individual, or focus on one person and every flower you choose has a meaning related to them.*

> *For the theme **relaxation** you could focus on a colour palette that is calming, or choose flowers with meanings you find restful and peaceful.*

MARY KELAVA

DAFFODIL

New beginnings

Events

Have you ever noticed how the most luxurious hotels, restaurants, and shops all have elegant floral displays to greet you when you come in the door? These places recognize the fact that flowers have a unique way of bringing a feeling of warmth and welcome to their environment. The flowers create a positive impact, visually and emotionally. The same holds true for special events.

There are many occasions throughout the year when a special event may be held. Sometimes they are for a personal reason and sometimes they are for a professional reason. But one thing they all have in common is that flowers are known to play a part in the big day.

Two of the biggest personal events are weddings and funerals. For both of these gatherings, flowers help create an atmosphere of life and beauty, but by using the language of flowers you will be able to personalise it with specific sentiments.

To give you some ideas, here is a list of meanings and flowers you may consider for a wedding and a list that might work well for a funeral.

Wedding

Adoration	*Sunflower*
Anticipation	*Anemone/Forsythia*
Dedication	*Hyacinth*
Devotion	*Alstroemeria/Lavender*
Eternal love	*Orange blossom/Rose (white)*
Everlasting love	*Baby's breath*
Friendship	*Alstroemeria/Freesia/Geranium/Rose (yellow)*
Happy life	*Peony*
Harmony	*Cosmos*
Love	*Carnation (red)/Myrtle/Rose/Rose (red)*
Loyalty	*Bamboo*
Marital happiness	*Stephanotis*
Marriage	*Myrtle*
New beginnings	*Daffodil*
Perfect happiness	*Rose (light pink)*
Perfect love	*Tulip*
Unity	*Allium*
Wedded love	*Ivy*

Sympathy

Comfort	*Ginger*
Eternal love	*Orange blossom/Rose (white)*
Everlasting love	*Baby's breath*
Goodbye	*Cyclamen*
Memories	*Periwinkle*
My thoughts are with you	*Calendula*
Peace	*Gardenia/Olive/Scabiosa*
Remembrance	*Forget-me-not/Poppy/Rosemary*
Sympathy	*Bee balm*
Thinking of you	*Pansy*
Thoughts of absent friends	*Zinnia*
Undying love	*Bleeding heart*
Warmth of feeling	*Mint*

In the professional world, fundraising galas and corporate parties bring large numbers of people together for a festive celebration. Using the language of flowers to represent a charity's or business's brand or mission is the perfect opportunity to create an even more memorable evening.

You can look at the following two examples of flowers and meanings for specific charity and corporate events to help you visualise what you may choose to do for your own.

Fundraising Gala for a New Hospital

Anticipation	*Anemone/Forsythia*
Appreciation	*Lisianthus*
Caring	*Tulip (pink)*
Generosity	*Peach blossom*
Goodwill to others	*Delphinium*
Gratitude	*Carnation (pink)/Lisianthus/ Rose (dark pink)*
Kindness	*Bluebell*
Support	*Lamb's ear*

Corporate Thank You Evening for Employees

Admiration	*Carnation/ Rose (red)*
Appreciation	*Lisianthus*
Dedication	*Hyacinth*
Devotion	*Alstroemeria/Lavender*
Gratitude	*Carnation (pink)/Lisianthus/Rose (dark pink)*
Prosperity	*Nigella*
Sincerity	*Fern/Hyacinth*
Thankfulness	*Rose (dark pink)*

If you are wondering what to do with all the flowers after your event, consider donating them.

If you go to the Bonus section and read **Repurposing Flowers**, you will learn about wonderful organisations that take donated flowers, rework them into individual bouquets, and deliver them to places in need of some beauty and joy.

MARY KELAVA

SWEET-PEA

Blissful pleasures/Thank you for a lovely time

A BOUQUET of WORDS

BLUEBELL

Kindness

PART II

Your Go-To Resources

A BOUQUET of WORDS

Just living is not enough . . . one must have sunshine, freedom, and a little flower.

—HANS CHRISTIAN ANDERSON

YOUR GO-TO RESOURCES

THIS CHAPTER INCLUDES YOUR most valuable resources for learning the language of flowers.

You will find the Flower Catalogue, Speciality Lists, and Helpful Tips straight from a former florist (me).

Flower Catalogue:

Flowers	31
Meanings	40

Speciality Lists:

Anniversary Years	52
Birth Months	55
Lunar New Year	58
Zodiac	61
The Significance of Colour	64
20 Flowers Readily Available All Year Long	65
15 of the Most Fragrant Flowers	67
12 Flowering Herbs	68
10 Popular Types of Greenery	69
10 Flowering House Plants	70
10 Flowering Garden Plants	71
10 of the Easiest Flowers to Grow from Seed	72
Flowers with More than One Common Name	73

Helpful Tips:

Floral Lingo	76
Arrangement	77
Smooth Delivery	78
Be Kind to Our Environment	79
Budget	81
Flower Care	82

FLOWER CATALOGUE

THIS IS YOUR GO-TO spot for finding flowers and their meanings.

There are two alphabetical lists for you to reference. The first is a list of flowers followed by their meanings, and the second is a list of meanings followed by the flowers that represent them.

You will find that you consult each list at different times for different reasons. For example, if you want to know the meaning of a specific flower, say *dahlia*, you will use the first list to quickly find the flower name, and then you will see the meaning: *dignity/elegance*. If you are looking for a specific sentiment, perhaps *thinking of you*, you will consult the second part of the list, find the meaning and then see any flowers that express that sentiment, in this case *pansy*.

A BOUQUET of Words

RANUNCULUS

Radiant Charm

Flowers

A

Allium—Good fortune/Unity

Alstroemeria—Devotion/Friendship

Amaranthus—Unfading love

Amaryllis—Splendid beauty

Anemone—Anticipation

Anthurium—Hospitality

Aster—Patience

Astilbe—Patience

Astrantia—Protection/Strength

Azalea—Fragile/Take care

B

Baby's breath—Everlasting love

Bamboo—Loyalty/Steadfastness

Basil—Best wishes

Bee balm—Sympathy

Begonia—Deep thoughts

Bells of Ireland—Good luck

Bird of Paradise—Magnificence

Bleeding heart—Undying love

Bluebell—Kindness

Borage—Courage

Bougainvillea—Passion/Welcome

Bouvardia—Enthusiasm

Buttercup—Cheerfulness

C

Calendula—Health/My thoughts are with you

Calla lily—Magnificent beauty

Camellia—Excellence

Carnation—Admiration/Affection

- ～ **pink**—gratitude/mother's love
- ～ **red**—love/passion
- ～ **white**—innocence/sweet & lovely

Cedar—Strength

Celosia—Affection

Chamomile—Energy in adversity

Cherry blossoms—Spiritual beauty

Chives—Usefulness

Chrysanthemum—Cheerfulness

Clematis—Mental beauty

Clove—Dignity

Clover—Good luck/Think of me

Cornflower—Hope in love

Cosmos—Harmony

Crocus—Cheerfulness/Joy

Cyclamen—Goodbye

D

Daffodil—New beginnings

Dahlia—Dignity/Elegance

Daisy—Innocence

Dandelion—Wishes

Delphinium—Cheer/Goodwill to others

- **blue (dark)**—dignity/grace
- **blue (light)**—youth/success
- **pink**—birth/new life
- **purple**—beauty
- **white**—youth

Dill—Good cheer/Good luck

Dogwood—Durability

E

Echinacea—Strength

Edelweiss—Courage

Eucalyptus—Protection

F

Fennel—Force/Strength

Fern—Shelter/Sincerity

Forget-me-not—Remembrance

Forsythia—Anticipation

Foxglove—Protection

Freesia—Friendship/Ultimate trust

Fritillaria—Majesty

Fuchsia—Amiability/Good taste

G

Gardenia—Peace/You are lovely

Geranium—Friendship

Gerbera—Cheerfulness

Ginger—Comfort/Warming

Gladiolus—Strength of character

H

Hawthorn—Hope

Heather—Protection

Hellebore—Balance

Hibiscus—Delicate beauty

Holly—Domestic happiness

Hollyhock—Ambition

Honeysuckle—Pure happiness

Hyacinth—Dedication/Sincerity

- ～ **blue**—constancy
- ～ **pink**—playfulness
- ～ **purple**—I'm sorry
- ～ **white**—loveliness

Hydrangea—Perseverance

I

Iris—Faith, hope, wisdom

- **blue**—faith/hope
- **purple**—royalty/wisdom
- **white**—purity
- **yellow**—passion

Ivy—Affection/Wedded love

J

Jasmine—Elegance/Grace

K

Kalanchoe—Endurance/Lasting affection

L

Larkspur—Levity/Lightness

Lamb's ear—Support

Lavender—Devotion

Lilac—First emotions of love

Lily—Beauty

Lily of the valley—Return to happiness/Sweetness

Lisianthus—Appreciation/Gratitude

Lupin—Imagination

M

Magnolia—Dignity

Marigold—Affection

Mimosa—Sensitivity

Mint—Warmth of feeling

Morning glory—Affection

Muscari—Tenderness

Myrtle—Love/Marriage

N

Narcissus—Renewal

Nasturtium—Victory in battle

Nigella—Independence/Prosperity

O

Olive—Peace

Orange blossom—Eternal love/Innocence

Oregano—Joy

Orchid—Refined beauty

P

Palm—Success/Victory

Pansy—Thinking of you

Peach blossom—Generosity

Peony—Happy life

Periwinkle—Memories/Sweet remembrance

Petunia—Your presence soothes me

Phlox—Agreement

Pine—Longevity

Plum blossom—Promise

Plumeria—Beauty/Grace

Poinsettia—Good cheer

Poppy—Remembrance/Restful sleep

Primrose—I can't live without you

Protea—Courage

R

Ranunculus—Radiant charm

Rose—Love

- **orange**—fascination
- **pink (dark)**—gratitude/thankfulness
- **pink (light)**—grace/perfect happiness
- **red**—admiration/love
- **white**—eternal love/innocence
- **yellow**—friendship/joy

Rosemary—Remembrance

S

Safflower—Welcome

Sage—Wisdom

Scabiosa—Peace/Purity

Snapdragon—Graciousness/Strength

Snowdrop—Hope

Solidago—Good luck

Star of Bethlehem—Atonement/Reconciliation

Stephanotis—Desire to travel/ Marital happiness

Stock—Lasting beauty

Strawflower—Agreement

Sunflower—Adoration

Sweet pea—Blissful pleasures/Thank you for a lovely time

Sweet William—Gallantry

T

Thistle—Protection

Thyme—Bravery/Courage

Tuberose—Pleasure

Tulip—Perfect love

- ∼ **orange**—enthusiasm
- ∼ **pink**—caring
- ∼ **purple**—elegance
- ∼ **red**—true love
- ∼ **white**—forgiveness
- ∼ **yellow**—there is sunshine in your smile

V

Violet—Faithfulness

W

Water lily—Purity of heart

Waxflower—Riches

Wisteria—Welcome

Y

Yarrow—Healing

Z

Zinnia—Thoughts of absent friends

Meanings

A

Admiration—Carnation/Rose (red)

Adoration—Sunflower

Affection—Carnation/Celosia/Ivy/Marigold/Morning glory

Agreement—Phlox/Strawflower

Ambition—Hollyhock

Amiability—Fuchsia

Anticipation—Anemone/Forsythia

Appreciation—Lisianthus

Atonement—Star of Bethlehem

B

Balance—Hellebore

Beauty—Delphinium (purple)/Lily/Plumeria

Best wishes—Basil

Birth—Delphinium (pink)

Blissful pleasures—Sweet pea

Bravery—Thyme

C

Caring—Tulip (pink)

Cheer—Delphinium

Cheerfulness—Buttercup/Chrysanthemum/Crocus/Gerbera

Comfort—Ginger

Constancy—Hyacinth (blue)

Courage—Borage/Edelweiss/Protea/Thyme

D

Dedication—Hyacinth

Deep thoughts—Begonia

Delicate beauty—Hibiscus

Desire to travel—Stephanotis

Devotion—Alstroemeria/Lavender

Dignity—Clove/Dahlia/Delphinium (dark blue)/Magnolia

Domestic happiness—Holly

Durability—Dogwood

E

Elegance—Dahlia/Jasmine/Tulip (purple)

Endurance—Kalanchoe

Energy in adversity—Chamomile

Enthusiasm—Bouvardia/Tulip (orange)

Eternal love—Orange blossom/Rose (white)

Everlasting love—Baby's breath

Excellence—Camellia

F

Faith—Iris (blue)

Faithfulness—Violet

Faith, hope, wisdom—Iris

Fascination—Rose (orange)
First emotions of love—Lilac
Force—Fennel
Forgiveness—Tulip (white)
Fragile—Azalea
Friendship—Alstroemeria/Freesia/Geranium/Rose (yellow)

G

Gallantry—Sweet William
Generosity—Peach blossom
Goodbye—Cyclamen
Good cheer—Dill/Poinsettia
Good fortune—Allium
Good luck—Bells of Ireland/Clover/Dill/Solidago
Good taste—Fuchsia
Goodwill to others—Delphinium
Grace—Delphinium (dark blue)/Jasmine/Plumeria/Rose (light pink)
Graciousness—Snapdragon
Gratitude—Carnation (pink)/Lisianthus/Rose (dark pink)

H

Happy life—Peony
Harmony—Cosmos
Healing—Yarrow
Health—Calendula

Hope—Hawthorn/Iris (blue)/Snowdrop

Hope in love—Cornflower

Hospitality—Anthurium

I

I can't live without you—Primrose

I'm sorry—Hyacinth (purple)

Imagination—Lupin

Independence—Nigella

Innocence—Carnation (white)/Daisy/Orange blossom/Rose (white)

J

Joy—Crocus/Oregano/Rose (yellow)

K

Kindness—Bluebell

L

Lasting affection—Kalanchoe

Lasting beauty—Stock

Levity—Larkspur

Lightness—Larkspur

Longevity—Pine

Love—Carnation (red)/Myrtle/Rose/Rose (red)

Loveliness—Hyacinth (white)

Loyalty—Bamboo

M

Magnificence—Bird of Paradise

Magnificent beauty—Calla lily

Majesty—Fritillaria

Marital happiness—Stephanotis

Marriage—Myrtle

Memories—Periwinkle

Mental beauty—Clematis

Mother's love—Carnation (pink)

My thoughts are with you—Calendula

N

New beginnings—Daffodil

New life—Delphinium (pink)

P

Passion—Bougainvillea/Carnation (red)/Iris (yellow)

Patience—Aster/Astilbe

Peace—Gardenia/Olive/Scabiosa

Perfect happiness—Rose (light pink)

Perfect love—Tulip

Perseverance—Hydrangea

Playfulness—Hyacinth (pink)

Pleasure—Tuberose

Promise—Plum blossom

Prosperity—Nigella

Protection—Astrantia/Eucalyptus/Foxglove/Heather/Thistle

Pure happiness—Honeysuckle

Purity—Iris (white)/Scabiosa

Purity of heart—Water lily

R

Radiant charm—Ranunculus

Reconciliation—Star of Bethlehem

Refined beauty—Orchid

Remembrance—Forget-me-not/Poppy/Rosemary

Renewal—Narcissus

Restful sleep—Poppy

Return to happiness—Lily of the valley

Riches—Waxflower

Royalty—Iris (purple)

S

Sensitivity—Mimosa

Sincerity—Fern/Hyacinth

Shelter—Fern

Spiritual beauty—Cherry blossoms

Splendid beauty—Amaryllis

Steadfastness—Bamboo

Strength—Astrantia/Cedar/Echinacea/Fennel/Snapdragon

Strength of character—Gladiolus

Success—Delphinium (light blue)/Palm

Support—Lamb's ear

Sweet & lovely—Carnation (white)

Sweetness—Lily of the valley

Sweet remembrance—Periwinkle

Sympathy—Bee balm

T

Take care—Azalea

Tenderness—Muscari

Thankfulness—Rose (dark pink)

Thank you for a lovely time—Sweet pea

There is sunshine in your smile—Tulip (yellow)

Thinking of you—Pansy

Think of me—Clover

Thoughts of absent friends—Zinnia

True love—Tulip (red)

U

Ultimate trust—Freesia

Undying love—Bleeding heart

Unfading love—Amaranthus

Unity—Allium

Usefulness—Chives

V

Victory—Palm

Victory in battle—Nasturtium

W

Warming—Ginger

Warmth of feeling—Mint

Wedded love—Ivy

Welcome—Bougainvillea/Safflower/Wisteria

Wisdom—Iris (purple)/Sage

Wishes—Dandelion

Y

You are lovely—Gardenia

Your presence soothes me—Petunia

Youth—Delphinium (light blue)/Delphinium (white)

A BOUQUET of WORDS

YELLOW ROSE

Friendship/Joy

SPECIALTY LISTS

SPECIALTY LISTS ARE FOCUSED on flowers and meanings for a specific topic and come in handy when you are learning the language of flowers, when you are short on time, or when you need a little extra inspiration.

Anniversary Years

Whether you're remembering your wedding day, the date a loved one passed away, how long it's been since you've kicked an addiction, or how many years you've been in business, what better way to celebrate an anniversary than with beautiful, meaningful flowers?

To mark the occasion in just the right way, start with the flower representing each anniversary year, then add in flowers that represent the sentiment you wish to express.

YEAR	FLOWER	SENTIMENT
1	Carnation	Admiration/Affection
	~Pink Carnation	Gratitude/mother's love
	~Red Carnation	Affection/love/passion
	~White Carnation	Innocence/sweet & lovely
2	Lily of the valley	Return to happiness/Sweetness
3	Sunflower	Adoration
4	Hydrangea	Perseverance
5	Daisy	Innocence
6	Calla lily	Magnificent beauty
7	Freesia	Friendship/Ultimate trust
8	Lilac	First emotions of love

YEAR	FLOWER	SENTIMENT
9	Bird of Paradise	Magnificence
10	Daffodil	New beginnings
11	Tulip	Perfect love
	~Orange Tulip	enthusiasm
	~Pink Tulip	Caring
	~Purple Tulip	Elegance
	~Red Tulip	True Love
	~White Tulip	Forgiveness
	~Yellow Tulip	There is sunshine in your smile
12	Peony	Happy LIfe
13	Chrysanthemum	Cheerfulness
14	Orchid	Refined Beauty
15	Rose	Love
	~Orange Rose	Fascination
	~Dark Pink Rose	Gratitude/Thankfulness
	~Light Pink Rose	Grace/Perfect Happiness
	~Red Rose	Admiration/Love
	~White Rose	Eternal Love/Innocence
	~Yellow Rose	Friendship/Joy

A BOUQUET OF WORDS

YEAR	FLOWER	SENTIMENT
20	Aster	Patience
25	Iris	Faith, Hope, Wisdom
	~Blue Iris	Faith/Hope
	~Purple Iris	Royalty/Wisdom
	~White Iris	Purity
	~Yellow Iris	Passion
30	Lily	Beauty
40	Gladiolus	Strength of Character
50	Yellow Rose	Friendship/Joy
	Violet	Faithfulness

Birth Months

Every month has one or two flowers designated to represent it. Surprise friends, family members, neighbours, and co-workers on their birthdays with their special flower.

January

Carnation—Admiration/Affection

- **pink**—gratitude/mother's love
- **red**—affection/love/passion
- **white**—innocence/sweet & lovely

Snowdrop—Hope

February

Primrose—I can't live without you

Violet—Faithfulness

March

Daffodil—New beginnings

April

Daisy—Innocence

Sweet pea—Blissful pleasures/Thank you for a lovely time

May

Hawthorn—Hope

Lily of the valley—Return to happiness/Sweetness

June

Honeysuckle—Pure happiness

Rose—Love

- **orange**—fascination
- **pink (dark)**—gratitude/thankfulness
- **pink (light)**—grace/perfect happiness
- **red**—admiration/love
- **white**—eternal love/innocence
- **yellow**—friendship/joy

July

Larkspur—Levity/Lightness

Water lily—Purity of heart

August

Gladiolus—Strength of character

Poppy—Remembrance/Restful sleep

September

Aster—Patience

Morning glory—Affection

October
Cosmos—Harmony

Marigold—Affection

November
Chrysanthemum—Cheerfulness

December
Narcissus—Renewal

Lunar New Year

Flowers play a key role when ringing in the Lunar New Year. There is a specific flower that brings luck for each of the zodiac characters, as well as other flowers with meanings that make them a perfect choice to celebrate the occasion.

Zodiac Characters

Rat

Lily—Beauty

Ox

Tulip—Perfect love

- **orange**—enthusiasm
- **pink**—caring; purple—elegance
- **red**—true love; white—forgiveness
- **yellow**—there is sunshine in your smile

Tiger

Anthurium—Hospitality

Rabbit

Snapdragon—Graciousness/Strength

Dragon

Hyacinth—Dedication/Sincerity

Snake

Orchid—Refined beauty

Horse

Jasmine—Elegance/Grace

Goat

Carnation—Admiration/Affection

- **pink**—gratitude/mother's love
- **red**—affection/love/passion
- **white**—innocence/sweet & lovely

Monkey

Chrysanthemum—Cheerfulness

Rooster

Gladiolus—Strength of character

Dog

Rose—Love

- **orange**—fascination
- **pink (dark)**—gratitude/thankfulness
- **pink (light)**—grace/perfect happiness
- **red**—admiration/love
- **white**—eternal love/innocence
- **yellow**—friendship/joy

Pig

Hydrangea—Perseverance

General

Anthurium—Hospitality

Bamboo—Loyalty/Steadfastness

Chrysanthemums—Cheerfulness

Gladiolus—Strength of character

Good fortune—Allium

Narcissus—Renewal

Orchid—Refined beauty

Peony—Happy life

Zodiac

Every star sign has a flower that represents it. These flowers make a great addition to a birthday bouquet.

Aries

March 21–April 19

Honeysuckle—Pure happiness

Taurus

April 20–May 20

Poppy—Remembrance/Restful sleep

Gemini

May 21–June 20

Lavender—Devotion

Cancer

June 21–July 22

White Rose—Eternal love/Innocence

Leo

July 23–August 22

Sunflower—Adoration

Virgo

August 23–September 22

Buttercup—Cheerfulness

Libra

September 23–October 22

Rose—Love

- **orange**—fascination
- **pink (dark)**—gratitude/thankfulness
- **pink (light)**—grace/perfect happiness
- **red**—admiration/love
- **white**—eternal love/innocence
- **yellow**—friendship/joy

Scorpio

October 23–November 21

Geranium—Friendship

Sagittarius

November 22–December 21

Carnation—Admiration/Affection

- **pink**—gratitude/mother's love
- **red**—affection/love/passion
- **white**—innocence/sweet & lovely

Capricorn
December 22–January 19
Pansy—Thinking of you

Aquarius
January 20–February 18
Orchid—Refined beauty

Pisces
February 19–March 20
Water lily—Purity of heart

The Significance of Colour

Every colour, from the deepest red to the palest purple, conveys a meaning and an emotion. Incorporating colour psychology into your flowers helps with the overall feeling and mood you are creating.

Red—Energy/Love/Passion/Strength

Orange—Enthusiasm/Joy/Warmth

Yellow—Cheerfulness/Joy/Optimism

Green—Energy/Freshness/Growth/Harmony/Life/Renewal

Blue—Calming/Serenity/Trust/Wisdom

Purple—Charm/Dignity/Elegance/Pride/Royalty/Success

Pink—Affection/Admiration/Compassion/Nurturing

White—Elegance/Innocence/Purity/Tranquillity

20 Flowers Readily Available All Year

Use this list to find the meanings for twenty flowers commonly available all year long.

Alstroemeria—Devotion/Friendship

Anthurium—Hospitality

Baby's breath—Everlasting love

Bells of Ireland—Good luck

Bird of Paradise—Magnificence

Calla lily—Magnificent beauty

- **Carnation**—Admiration/Affection
- **pink**—gratitude/mother's love
- **red**—love/passion
- **white**—innocence/sweet & lovely

Chamomile—Energy in adversity

Chrysanthemum—Cheerfulness

Freesia—Friendship/Ultimate trust

Gerbera—Cheerfulness

Gladiolus—Strength of character

Hydrangea—Perseverance

Lily—Beauty

Lisianthus—Appreciation/Gratitude

Orchid—Refined beauty

Rose—Love

- **orange**—fascination
- **pink (dark)**—gratitude/thankfulness
- **pink (light)**—grace/perfect happiness
- **red**—admiration/love
- **white**—eternal love/innocence
- **yellow**—friendship/joy

Snapdragon—Graciousness/Strength

Solidago—Good luck

Waxflower—Riches

15 of the Most Fragrant Flowers

The fragrance of a specific flower can create a memory so strong it can be recalled decades later. Here are 15 of the most fragrant flowers:

Freesia—Friendship/Ultimate trust

Gardenia—Peace/You are lovely

Honeysuckle—Pure happiness

Jasmine—Elegance/Grace

Lavender—Devotion

Lilac—First emotions of love

Lily—Beauty

Lily of the Valley—Return to happiness/Sweetness

Orange blossom—Eternal love/Innocence

Plumeria—Beauty/Grace

Roses—Love

- **orange**—fascination
- **pink (dark)**— gratitude/thankfulness
- **pink (light)**—grace/perfect happiness
- **red**—admiration/love

Stephanotis—Desire to travel/Marital happiness

Stock—Lasting beauty

Sweet pea—Blissful pleasures/Thank you for a lovely time

Tuberose—Pleasure

12 Flowering Herbs

There are many flowering herbs that can be included in bouquets. Have fun experimenting with the ones in this list.

Basil—Best wishes

Bee balm—Sympathy

Borage—Courage

Chive—Usefulness

Clove—Dignity

Dill—Good cheer/Good luck

Fennel—Force/Strength

Mint—Warmth of feeling

Oregano—Joy

Rosemary—Remembrance

Sage—Wisdom

Thyme—Bravery/Courage

10 Popular Types of Greenery

Not only do various types of greenery play an important role in bouquets and flower arrangements to make them visually appealing, but their meanings can help you convey the exact message you want.

Bamboo—Loyalty/Steadfastness

Cedar—Strength

Eucalyptus—Protection

Fern—Shelter/Sincerity

Ivy—Affection/Wedded love

Lamb's ear—Support

Myrtle—Love/Marriage

Olive—Peace

Palm—Success/Victory

Pine—Longevity

10 Flowering Houseplants

In this list you will find ten of the most common flowering houseplants and their meanings. All make great gifts.

African Violet—Faithfulness

Anthurium—Hospitality

Begonia—Deep thoughts

Cyclamen—Goodbye

Jasmine—Elegance/Grace

Kalanchoe—Endurance/Lasting affection

Orchid—Refined beauty

Lily—Beauty

Poinsettia—Good cheer

Rose—Love

- ∼ **orange**—fascination
- ∼ **pink (dark)**—gratitude/thankfulness
- ∼ **pink (light)**—grace/perfect happiness
- ∼ **red**—admiration/love
- ∼ **white**—eternal love/innocence
- ∼ **yellow**—friendship/joy

10 Flowering Garden Plants

Reference this list to find the meanings for ten of the most popular flowering garden plants.

Camelia—Excellence

Geranium—Friendship

Hellebore—Balance

Hibiscus—Delicate beauty

Hydrangea—Perseverance

Lavender—Devotion

Marigold—Affection

Pansy—Thinking of you

Petunia—Your presence soothes me

Rose—Love

- **orange**—fascination
- **pink (dark)**—gratitude/thankfulness
- **pink (light)**—grace/perfect happiness
- **red**—admiration/love
- **white**—eternal love/innocence
- **yellow**—friendship/joy

10 of the Easiest Flowers to Grow from Seed

Not all of us are gardening experts—me included—so here is a list of easy-to-grow flowers for any beginners out there.

Calendula—Health/My thoughts are with you

Cornflower—Hope in love

Cosmos—Harmony

Marigold—Affection

Nasturtium—Victory in battle

Nigella—Independence/Prosperity

Poppy—Remembrance/Restful sleep

Sunflower—Adoration

Sweet pea—Blissful pleasures/Thank you for a lovely time

Zinnia—Thoughts of absent friends

Flowers with More than one Common Name

Flowers tend to have a botanical name and then the more common name that we are familiar with. But some flowers also have a second common name or a frequently used nickname. Here are a few:

Amaranthus—Love lies bleeding (Unfading love)

Chrysanthemum—Mums (Cheerfulness)

Cornflower—Bachelor's button (Hope in love)

Echinacea—Coneflower (Strength)

Gladiolus—Glads (Strength of character)

Muscari—Grape hyacinth (Tenderness)

Nigella—Love-in-a-mist (Independence/Prosperity)

Solidago—Goldenrod (Good luck)

A BOUQUET of Words

DAHLIA

Dignity/Elegance

HELPFUL TIPS

WITHIN ALL INDUSTRIES THERE are things you're not aware of unless you are in that line of work, and the floral industry is no different. Here are some things I learned as a florist that I think will be helpful for you to know.

Floral Lingo

Knowing just a few key floral terms will help you avoid potential confusion and/or disappointment when placing an order with your local florist.

In my experience as a florist, I found when customers were ordering flowers, the majority would ask me for a 'flower arrangement'. I quickly learned that I needed to clarify exactly what it was they were looking for as more often than not it was a *bouquet* they wanted, not an *arrangement*. Here is a breakdown of what bouquets and arrangements are, as well as the benefits of each.

Bouquet

A bouquet is a group of carefully arranged flowers and greenery that is usually presented wrapped. There is no vase.

Most bouquets come in a round shape, but they can also be created in a presentation style, which is longer and thinner, perfect for holding in the crook of your arm.

Benefits of a bouquet:

- Since there is no vase, the money you spend is all for flowers.
- A bouquet is easy for you to carry home or deliver.
- Whoever receives the bouquet gets a chance to reuse one of the vases they already own.

Arrangement

An arrangement is a selection of flowers and greenery that has been designed in a container. Vases, jugs, Mason jars, plastic-lined baskets, or even teapots can be used. Just make sure whatever is used can hold water or add a leak-proof lining to it.

An arrangement can be designed to be either *front-facing* or *all-around*.

A front-facing arrangement has the majority of flowers on one side, making it look nice and full, while the back is quite flat. This is perfect when the arrangement is going to be placed on a mantelpiece or on a table/counter against a wall.

An all-around arrangement looks equally full from all angles. This style is used when being placed in the middle of a table.

If you're not sure where the flowers will be displayed, it's best to choose the all-around style.

Benefits of an arrangement:

- There's no need to find a vase to put the flowers in, as the arrangement comes ready to be put on display.
- A container can be chosen to enhance the overall look and feeling of the arrangement.
- The container you choose can become a keepsake, something to use over and over again.

Smooth Delivery

I never grew tired of the look of delight on someone's face as they received the flowers I was delivering. Unfortunately, at the beginning of my career, some deliveries did not go as smoothly as they should have because I would be missing a key piece of information.

To make sure the flowers you order are delivered successfully, give the florist as much detail as possible. Include the following:

- The recipient's name, address, and phone number.
- Buzzer number if one is needed for access.
- Your name and phone number.
- Hours of operation for an office/business (it's also very helpful to find out if they close for a lunch hour).
- Where the flowers can be left if the recipient isn't at home/work.
- Any other information you think might be helpful (e.g., *Their doorbell isn't working, so please knock on the door.*) and that will make the delivery go smoothly.

Be Kind to Our Environment

It's not the most natural thing in the world to think of the floral industry causing harm to the environment, but this is in fact the case. Over the years there have been some bad practices, but the good news is, there are more and more florists actively working towards positive change. Here are some things that will help you to make environmentally friendly choices when choosing flowers.

- Shop local: While all flowers are beautiful, the absolute cream of the crop are those grown locally. The flowers have had less handling, less refrigeration, and less time in storage than those shipped in from around the world. They are grown and harvested in their natural blooming season, giving you flowers that are fresher, more fragrant, and longer lasting.

- Request eco-friendly materials: Two of the main flower shop problems regarding environmentally friendly materials are the high volume of single use plastic waste and the use of floral foam.

- It has become an acceptable practice for florists to wrap bouquets in cellophane. Once the flowers reach their destination, that wrapper is tossed straight into the trash. Instead, ask your florist to wrap the flowers in brown paper or another recyclable material, decline any wrapping, or bring in a vase you already have to be reused.

A BOUQUET OF WORDS

- Floral foam is that green, sponge-like material used in containers to hold flower stems in place. It is non-biodegradable, non-recyclable, and toxic. Find a florist who uses natural materials such as sticks, stones, sand, or moss, as an armature.

Budget

One of the things I love most about using the language of flowers is that no matter what your budget is, you can absolutely create the floral message you want within your price range. A single stem, an abundant bouquet, or anything in between can all be successful at sharing your sentiments.

These are my top two tips on how to make the most of your flowers to stretch your budget:

1. Buy a large bouquet and divide it up into small bunches so then you can have a vase of flowers in every room.

2. 'Downsize' your arrangement (my mum is the queen of doing this). Not all flowers last the same amount of time, so as one flower in the vase wilts, remove it. You can keep doing this until all you have is a single stem in a bud vase. Downsizing like this will keep the overall look of your flowers as fresh as possible, for as long as possible.

Flower Care

Flowers are a perishable product, but there are some things you can do to enjoy them for the longest time possible:

- Make sure to start with a clean vase. Any bacteria in your vase will shorten the life of the flowers.

- Change the water in your vase every two days. Fresh water is very important. It only takes a minute to do but makes a huge difference in how long your flowers stay fresh.

- Cut the flower stems at an angle to have the largest surface area through which water can be absorbed.

- When displaying your flowers, keep them away from direct sunlight and drafts. It's also important to keep them away from fresh fruit, as the ethylene gas the fruit emits is detrimental to flowers.

- To keep your arrangement fresh and healthy, remove each bloom as it fades.

- Flower food: The little packets of flower food the florist gives you are good for nourishing the flowers and keeping bacteria at bay, but only if you follow the directions correctly. If you don't mix the right amount of food with the right amount of water it could do more harm than good. It's best to skip using the flower food if you don't know the correct measurements.

MARY KELAVA

POPPY

Remembrance/Restful sleep

PART III

'Remember Forever' Space

*All of the flowers of all the tomorrows
are in the seeds of today.*

—INDIAN PROVERB

REMEMBER FOREVER SPACE

THIS IS WHERE YOU can document your ideas, your actions, and the flower-giving dates that are important to you. This will be a great resource for you to look back on throughout the year and in years to come. I have divided it into three parts: Notes, Records, and Calendars.

Notes:

Note Pages	89

Gift Records:

Record Your Gifts	95

Calendars:

Flower Gift Giving Dates	101
National Flower Dates	107
Personal Calendar	114

A BOUQUET of Words

DAISY

Innocence

NOTES

Think of these pages as a place to jot down any useful thoughts, ideas, comments or reminders. This could be when someone tells you their favourite flower or colour, when their birthday is, a flower you've seen that you want to remember the name of, or maybe a word you've thought of to describe a specific person—anything you think will be a useful reference throughout the year.

NOTES

NOTES

NOTES

NOTES

A BOUQUET of Words

LILY OF THE VALLEY

Return to happiness/Sweetness

GIFT RECORDS

This is the place for you to record your actions. Make note of who you gave flowers to, why you gave them, when you gave them, what flowers you chose, and what message you sent.

WHO DID YOU SEND THEM TO?	DATE
WHY DID YOU SEND THEM?	
FLOWERS SENT:	
MESSAGE INCLUDED:	

WHO DID YOU SEND THEM TO?	DATE
WHY DID YOU SEND THEM?	
FLOWERS SENT:	
MESSAGE INCLUDED:	

A BOUQUET OF WORDS

GIFT RECORDS

WHO DID YOU SEND THEM TO?	DATE
WHY DID YOU SEND THEM?	
FLOWERS SENT:	
MESSAGE INCLUDED:	

WHO DID YOU SEND THEM TO?	DATE
WHY DID YOU SEND THEM?	
FLOWERS SENT:	
MESSAGE INCLUDED:	

GIFT RECORDS

WHO DID YOU SEND THEM TO?	DATE
WHY DID YOU SEND THEM?	
FLOWERS SENT:	
MESSAGE INCLUDED:	

WHO DID YOU SEND THEM TO?	DATE
WHY DID YOU SEND THEM?	
FLOWERS SENT:	
MESSAGE INCLUDED:	

A BOUQUET of WORDS

CHRYSANTHEMUM

Cheerfulness

MARY KELAVA

CALENDARS
HERE ARE THREE CALENDARS to help keep track of flowery moments throughout the year.

A BOUQUET of Words

CLEMATIS

Mental beauty

Flower Gift Giving Dates

Throughout the year there are many opportunities to give flowers. These could be times that happen annually, such as birthdays, anniversaries, Valentine's Day or Mother's Day, or they could be one-time events, such as congratulating someone on their new home, welcoming a new baby, or sending get-well wishes. Each opportunity gives you the chance to use the language of flowers. Here are some of the more notable dates throughout the year, with suggestions on how you can incorporate flowers into that day.

New Year's Day

January 1—Make your New Year's resolution to have a flower-filled year. This can include having flowers in your own home, gifting flowers to others, or perhaps starting your very own flower garden (even if that means pots on your patio).

Blue Monday

Blue Monday—**the third Monday in January**—has been labelled the most depressing day of the year. I suggest fighting this by buying some flowers—blue ones if you can. Only 10% of flowers come in the colour blue, but the ones you can get are sure to benefit your mental, physical and emotional wellbeing. Blue flowers are known to produce a calming effect that in turn slows down our metabolism and thoughts. Here are some blue flowers that are sure to delight you: cornflower (hope in love), delphinium (cheer/goodwill to others), forget-me-not (remembrance), hydrangea (perseverance), and nigella (independence/prosperity).

Lunar New Year

Lunar New Year begins on the New Moon that appears between **January 21** and **February 20**.

In the Chinese Zodiac there is a specific flower that brings luck for each of the zodiac signs. Not only can you use these flowers to help celebrate Lunar New Year, but they make a great choice as part of a flower arrangement for a new-born baby or birthday gift.

See Speciality List **Lunar Zodiac Flowers**.

Valentine's Day

February 14—While the red rose (admiration/love) is the flower that's given the most for Valentine's Day, there are other flowers that are appropriate to give on this day. My suggestions are: calla lily (magnificent beauty), carnation (admiration/affection), freesia (friendship/ultimate trust), orchid (refined beauty), primrose (I can't live without you), sunflower (adoration), tulip (perfect love), and yellow tulip (there is sunshine in your smile).

Random Acts of Kindness Day

February 17—Growing in popularity, Random Acts of Kindness Day is celebrated by individuals, groups, and organisations to encourage acts of kindness. Giving flowers on this day to those you know—or a complete stranger—is one way you can participate and make someone else's day a little bit brighter.

International Women's Day

Recognized on **March 8**, the official flower for International Women's Day is the mimosa (sensitivity). It was chosen by feminists in Italy to represent this day, as a symbol of strength for women.

Easter

Easter occurs on a Sunday between **March 22** and **April 25**. We're spoiled for choices when it comes to choosing flowers at Easter time. All the spring blooms bring a freshness and sense of lightness and hope after the long winter. While the Easter lily (beauty) is the iconic flower to represent the day, consider other seasonal choices, such as crocus (cheerfulness/joy), daffodil (new beginnings), olive (peace), and snowdrop (hope).

Earth Day

April 22—Earth Day began in 1970 as a day to raise awareness of the importance of protecting the natural resources of the planet for generations to come. A common practice on this day is to plant a tree. Another tradition you can begin is to plant a flower. Choosing one with significance to you would make it extra special.

Mother's Day

Mother's Day is celebrated in Canada and the US on the **second Sunday in May**. In the UK, Mothering Sunday is celebrated on the **fourth Sunday in Lent** (this is usually in March).

Many people think Valentine's Day is the busiest time of the year for florists, but actually it's just edged out of top place by the day we celebrate our mums!

The official flower for Mother's Day is the carnation. A pink carnation is especially appropriate as it has the meaning of 'Mother's love'.

Father's Day

Celebrated on the **third Sunday of June**, the official flower for Father's Day is the rose—red or white. A red rose symbolises a father who is still living, while a white rose honours one who has passed away.

Thanksgiving

Canada: October—**2nd Monday**

US: November—**4th Thursday**

Lisianthus (appreciation/gratitude), pink carnations (gratitude), and dark pink roses (gratitude/thankfulness) are all great floral choices to celebrate Thanksgiving. If you're a guest at someone's house for the occasion, think of giving a gift of anthurium (hospitality) or sweet peas (thank you for a lovely time).

Remembrance Day

November 11—The poppy (restful sleep/remembrance) is the official symbol for Remembrance Day, but there are other flowers you can choose to create a special message. Think of thyme to represent bravery, sweet William for gallantry, periwinkle for memories, and calendula to say my thoughts are with you.

Christmas

December 25—As Christmas falls in the dead of winter, you may not think of decorating with fresh flowers, but they make a great addition to your more traditional decor. Flowers bring a wonderful sense of freshness into your home and make an even bigger impact when paired with fragrant seasonal greenery. Choosing meaningful flowers to celebrate this holiday season will make your home shine even brighter.

A BOUQUET of Words

HYDRANGEA

Perseverance

National Flower Dates

These are great days to recognise to help you have a flower-filled year:

January 10: National Houseplant Appreciation Day

Quick list '10 Flowering House Plants'

January—3rd Saturday: National Tulip Day

Tulip—Perfect love

- **orange**—enthusiasm
- **pink**—caring
- **purple**—elegance
- **red**—true love
- **white**—forgiveness
- **yellow**—there is sunshine in your smile

January 28: National Daisy Day

Daisy—Innocence

January 29: National Carnation Day

Carnation—Admiration/Affection

- **pink**—gratitude/mother's love
- **red**—affection/love/passion
- **white**—innocence/sweet & lovely

January—Last Saturday: National Seed Swap Day

Speciality List '10 of the Easiest Flowers to Grow from Seed'

February 7: Rose Day

Rose—Love

- **Orange**—fascination
- **pink (dark)**—gratitude/thankfulness
- **pink (light)**—grace/perfect happiness
- **red**—admiration/love
- **white**—eternal love/innocence
- **yellow**—friendship/joy

February 28: National Floral Design Day

Speciality List '20 Flowers Readily Available All Year Long'

March 3: National Peach Blossom Day

Peach blossom—Generosity

March 12: Plant a Flower Day

Speciality List '10 Flowering Garden Plants'

March 21: National Fragrance Day

Speciality List '15 of the Most Fragrant Flowers'

April 5: National Dandelion Day

Dandelion—Wishes

April 6: California Poppy Day

Poppy—Remembrance/Restful sleep

April 16: National Orchid Day

Orchid—Refined beauty

April 19: National Primrose Day

Primrose—I can't live without you

April 28: Crocus Day

Crocus—Cheerfulness/Joy

May—First Sunday: National Herb Day

Speciality List '12 Flowering Herbs'

May— First Friday: National Flower Arranging Day

Speciality List 'Flower Care'

May—2nd Sunday: Lilac Sunday

Lilac—First emotions of love

May 4: Greenery Day

Speciality List '10 Popular Types of Greenery'

May 8: Iris Day

Iris—Faith, hope, wisdom

- **blue**—faith/hope
- **purple**—royalty/wisdom
- **white**—purity
- **yellow**—passion

May 30: Water a Flower day

Speciality List '10 Flowering House Plants'

June 12: National Red Rose Day

Red Rose—Admiration/Love

June 27: National Orange Blossom Day

Orange blossom—Eternal love/Innocence

September 18: World Bamboo Day

Bamboo—Loyalty/Steadfastness

November 10: Forget-me-not Day

Forget-me-not—Remembrance

December 12: Poinsettia Day

Poinsettia—Good cheer

December 19: National Holly Day

Holly—Domestic happiness

A BOUQUET OF WORDS

DANDELION

Wishes

PERSONAL CALENDAR

THIS BLANK CALENDAR IS for you to personalise with all the birthdays, anniversaries, and special reasons to celebrate in your life.

A Bouquet of Words

JANUARY

FEBRUARY

MARCH

APRIL

MAY

JUNE

JULY

AUGUST

A BOUQUET OF WORDS

SEPTEMBER

OCTOBER

NOVEMBER

DECEMBER

NOTES

A BOUQUET OF WORDS

RED CARNATION

Love/Passion

PART IV

AND THERE'S MORE

A BOUQUET OF WORDS

Even if the flower is no more, still, the fragrance can be.

—JAGGI VASUDER
(INDIAN YOGI AND AUTHOR)

AND THERE'S MORE

THIS SECTION INCLUDES BONUS lists on floral related topics, answers to frequently asked questions, and just a little bit about me.

Bonus Lists

There are many great things to learn about flowers. While my focus for *A Bouquet of Words* was showing how and why to express yourself through the language of flowers, I also wanted to share with you some *bonus lists* on other flower-related topics.

Edible Flowers	123
Preserving Flowers	125
Flower Tourism	128
Floral Baby Names and Their Meanings	130
No Fresh Flowers—No Problem	131
Repurposing Flowers	134

Edible Flowers

Edible flowers have an almost magical quality. They transform even the simplest cuisine into something special.

Fresh petals sprinkled over your culinary creation provide a pleasing aesthetic that puts a smile on faces, while using dried flowers in your baking or savoury dishes adds a unique hint of flavour that is sure to be a delight.

Safety

Before you decide to 'up your cooking game' by grabbing a handful of flowers from your garden or picking some petals off that beautiful bouquet you just received, remember—*not all flowers are edible!* When using flowers in your dishes, there are some important things you need to consider. Here are three safety tips for you to remember:

1. **Never assume a flower is edible.** The first thing you need to do is identify the flower *exactly*. There are lists online that you can use to find out what varieties of flowers are edible. If, after checking a list, you're still in doubt, don't use it.

2. **Clean your blossoms.** Whether you've picked flowers from your garden, bought them from a farmer, or purchased them from a store, wash and pat dry your flowers before use.

3. **Be aware of allergies.** While flowers are a great addition to your cooking and baking, they're still considered a danger to those with allergies. Always check with your guests before serving.

Some of my favourite edible flowers

Pansy—while pansies can be used in a salad, they are more widely used candied to decorate baking. They don't have a strong flavour, but have a hint of garden-fresh.

Nasturtium—one of the most popular edible flowers. All parts except the seed are edible and have a peppery radish taste to them.

Borage—this dainty, star-shaped flower most often comes in the colour blue. It has a cooling cucumber-like taste and makes a lovely garnish for salads, cheese plates, sweet treats, and summer drinks.

Calendula—a subtle flavour that ranges from peppery to bitter, making them a great addition to soups and salads. Their bright yellow, gold, or orange petals can be used to tint custard, egg, and rice dishes.

Violet—the pretty purple petals have a hint of mint, making them a perfect garnish for sweet or savoury dishes.

Rose—the most flavourful rose petals are those that are the most fragrant. They are great to infuse liquids, garnish baked goods, or as an addition to salads.

Dandelion—if you want to eat something packed full of nutrients, look no further than the humble dandelion. Young dandelions have a sweet, almost honey taste, changing to a more bitter taste as they mature.

Hibiscus—these colourful, tropical flowers are mostly used for making tea or a flavour-filled syrup.

Preserving Flowers

Sometimes flowers are so special you want them to last forever. Here are the two easiest and most popular ways you can make that happen:

Drying

A classic method of flower preservation; here are the steps to follow:

1. If your flowers have been in water, take a soft cloth and dry the stems. Moisture is the enemy of flower preservation so it's best to get rid of what you can before you begin. I also give the ends of the stems a fresh trim.

2. Choose a few stems and tie them together. Ventilation is key here so it's better to tie just a few together and have several smaller bunches than one big bunch. I also like to vary the length of the stems to give as much room for air to circulate as possible.

3. Now it's time to hang your flowers upside down to dry. The important thing in this step is to find a dark, dry area because while drying flowers will fade their colour, darkness will help minimise this fading.

4. Leave the bunches hanging for 2–3 weeks and then check on them. If you detect no moisture, untie them.

5. Your beautifully preserved flowers are ready to use. You could pop the flowers into a vase to create a striking ar-

rangement; pull the petals off the stems, mix them in a clear glass bowl with dried herbs and spices and add a couple of drops of essential oil to make a fragrant potpourri; or form them into a wreath to hang on your door for a year-round decoration.

Pressing

While you can buy a flower 'press' to do the job, pressing flowers between the pages of a book can also give you the results you're looking for. Here's what you need to know:

1. Collect your materials: Flowers, absorbent paper, and a heavy book. (Choose any thin, porous paper—paper towels and tissue paper both work well.)

2. Lay one sheet of paper inside the pages of a heavy book. Place your flowers face down on the paper, leaving lots of space around each one, and then cover with the second piece of paper. (When covering the flowers with the second piece of paper, be very careful. You want to make sure all the petals of the flowers stay flat. If you move too quickly you may disturb your layout.)

3. Carefully close your book and place it between other heavy books, leaving it undisturbed for at least two weeks. When you check your flowers, if they aren't completely dry, close the book, leave for another week, and check again. (You'll know they are ready when they have a papery feeling to them.)

4. Your pressed flowers are perfect for a whole host of DIY projects. You can use them to make greeting cards, bookmarks, wrapping paper, jewellery, wall hangings, coasters—there's really no limit to what you can do to personalise your home décor or create unique gifts for family and friends.

Flower Tourism

Let me introduce you to flower tourism—specifically planning your travels to see flowers around the world. There are many destinations that boast spectacular displays of wild or cultivated flowers. Here are a few to put on your wish list:

Holland

Flower: Tulip

Meaning: Perfect love

orange—enthusiasm

pink—caring

purple—elegance

red—true love

white—forgiveness

yellow—there is sunshine in your smile

Best time to visit: Mid-April

Provence

Flower: Lavender

Meaning—Devotion

Best time to visit: Early to mid-July

England

Flower: Bluebells

Meaning—Kindness

Best time to visit: Mid-April to late May

Azores

Flower: Hydrangea

Meaning—Perseverance

Best time to visit: Mid-August

California

Flower: Poppies

Meaning—Remembrance/Restful sleep

Best time to visit: Mid-March to late May

TO NOTE: *Best time to visit* is based on the time of year the flowers have historically been in bloom. However, each year times may vary depending on weather and growing conditions.

Floral Baby Names and Their Meanings

- Aster—Patience
- Clover—Good luck/Think of me
- Daisy—Innocence
- Fern—Shelter/Sincerity
- Ginger—Comfort/Warming
- Heather—Protection
- Holly—Domestic happiness
- Iris—Faith, hope, wisdom
- Ivy—Affection/Wedded love
- Jasmine—Elegance/Grace
- Lily—Beauty
- Marigold—Affection
- Nigella—Independence/Prosperity
- Olive—Peace
- Poppy—Remembrance/Restful sleep
- Rose—Love
- Rosemary—Remembrance
- Sage—Wisdom
- Violet—Faithfulness

No Fresh Flowers—No Problem

Sometimes when you are using the language of flowers, you know just what flower you want to use to create your message but can't find it in its fresh form. If you run into that situation don't worry, I have several suggestions for other ways you can include that particular flower.

Greeting card: Greeting cards are an excellent way to include a difficult-to-find flower. For example, if you know someone with a July birthday and want to include their birth month flower of water lily (purity of heart), you would find it near impossible to find a fresh one. Instead, represent the birth month flower by giving a card with the image of a water lily on the front.

Edible: Edible flowers are becoming more popular every year. While during their growing season fresh edible flowers are readily available (marigold-affection; nasturtium-victory in battle; pansy-thinking of you), during the rest of the year you'll need to turn to other options. You can buy jars of dried flowers (rose-love; lavender-devotion; borage-courage), as well as many floral teas (chamomile-energy in adversity; echinacea-strength; hibiscus-delicate beauty).

Poetry: Think of sharing a poem to express your sentiment. I always think of this line from William Wordsworth's poem 'I Wandered Lonely as a Cloud':

> "...When all at once I saw a crowd,
> A host, of golden daffodils..."

With this example, you could represent 'new beginnings' (daffodils) no matter what time of the year it is.

Another option is to try writing your own poem with a floral theme. What a heartfelt way to make meaningful connections with others!

Artwork: Monet, Van Gough, O'Keefe—all have famous floral paintings. But you don't need to go with someone famous to have beautiful artwork of flowers. See what local artists have to offer. With the wide range of styles and prices, you have a good chance of finding just what you are looking for.

Jewellery: Necklaces, rings, earrings—whatever type of jewellery you're looking for, you're sure to find something with a flower on it. One of my favourite necklaces is of my birth month flower. It is a silver snowdrop (hope) with a peridot gemstone tucked in the middle of the dainty petals. I bought this from a local artist, but I also love seeing what I can find when I go on holidays in a different country.

Scented bath and beauty products: I have an array of floral-scented bath and beauty products at home. Plumeria, lavender, rose, freesia, honeysuckle, jasmine, orange blossom—the list goes on. For me, if a bath or beauty product is going to be scented, make it a floral one.

Scented candles: What's better than filling a room with a beautiful floral fragrance? While some candles have the distinct fragrance of a specific flower, many floral scented candles are often mixed with other scents such as fruit or spices. I prefer the purity of a fragrance from one flower, but test a few different kinds to see what resonates with you.

Packets of flower seeds: A packet of flower seeds makes a lovely little gift. The seeds are inexpensive and you can just slip the packet in a card and pop it in the mail for the price of a regular stamp. One of my favourite packets of seeds to send is the pansy (thinking of you). I also like to put a packet of poppy seeds (remembrance/restful sleep) in a sympathy card.

Check the Specialty Lists *15 of the Most Fragrant Flowers* and *10 of the Easiest Flowers to Grow from Seed* for information you may find useful.

Repurposing Flowers

There are some truly great "floral angels" out there who volunteer their time to pick up donated flowers, repurpose them into bouquets, and deliver them to places in their city in need of some joy and beauty. Here are some of the organisations:

Bouquets of Aloha: Maui, Hawaii

> *Mission: "To bring joy and kindness to those in need and a new life to flowers."*

Bouquets of Aloha accepts donated flowers and restyles them into bouquets which are then delivered to the elderly in senior centres.

Bouquets of Kindness: Northeast Florida

> *"Strengthening our community, showing kindness to our neighbours and growing friendship in unexpected places with the gift of flowers."*

Bouquets of Kindness accepts donated flowers and then takes them, tools and supplies to senior living facilities. The Bouquets of Kindness volunteers stay and encourage the seniors to create their own arrangements.

FlowerRescue: Helsinki

> *Vision: "No flower goes to waste before bringing joy to someone."*

FlowerRescue collects surplus flowers from those in the floral industry and repurposes them into bouquets they then deliver to residents, hospitals, and charity partners.

Petals for Hope: All US States

> *Mission: "To help transform the event and wedding industry into a more sustainable one by creating a streamlined and cost-effective donation process."*

Petals for Hope repurposes donated flowers from floral events and businesses by restyling them into bedside bouquets and arrangements. These are then delivered to those in the community in need. They also use the flower donations to host floral arranging workshops for children's hospitals, nursing homes, at-risk children, and shelters.

Random Acts of Flowers: Knoxville/Tampa Bay/Indianapolis

> *Vision: "Our vision as a flower charity is to inspire and nurture a culture of care and compassion."*

Random Acts of Flowers delivers "recycled flowers, encouragement and personal moments of kindness" to improve the emotional health and wellbeing of individuals in healthcare facilities.

Rebloom Flowers: Across Canada

> *Mission: "To ensure flowers are enjoyed for days, not hours, and our environment doesn't suffer from enjoyment of them."*

Rebloom uses a three-step process: Step1- Pick up flowers that would otherwise end up in the garbage and redesign them into bedside table arrangements; Step 2—Deliver newly redesigned flowers to a charity of your choice; Step 3—Compost the flowers when the flowers have reached the end of their life span. (Note: Rebloom charges for their pick up and compost service.)

The Reflower Project: Boston and South Shore, MA areas

> *Goal: "To be 'green', and we are dedicated to improving the health of the environment and wellbeing of our community."*

The Reflower Project re-purposes and delivers flowers to community centres.

The Floral Project: UK

> *Goal: "Sow, grow, and give cut flowers to those in their community that need a smile."*

The Floral Project has gardeners—experienced and new—all around the UK creating a cut flower patch in their own garden as a way to grow flowers and give to those in their community.

The Growing Kindness Project

Began in Washington State and now expanding nationally and internationally.

> *Goal: "To start a campaign of kindness that starts a ripple of goodwill that reaches across the world."*

The Growing Kindness Project provides support, education, and resources to those wanting to share kindness by growing and giving flowers.

If you can't find an organisation in your area, consider reaching out to some places in your neighbourhood where you could brighten someone's day with your floral donation.

A BOUQUET of Words

WATER LILY

Purity of heart

FAQs

HERE YOU WILL FIND answers to some of the most common questions you might have. If you don't find your answer here, please feel free to reach out to me through my website.

What is the *Flower Catalogue*?

The flower catalogue is a master list containing all the flowers and meanings included in this book. The list has two parts, one with the flower names first followed by their meanings and one with the meanings listed first. Both are in alphabetical order. There are two lists because sometimes you know the name of a flower and want to look up its meaning, while at other times you know what meaning you want to share and are looking to find the flowers to match it.

What are *Speciality Lists*?

Speciality lists are helpful lists related to a specific topic. You'll find them a quick source of information.

I don't have a big budget. Am I still able to create meaningful flowers?

Yes! Part of the beauty of using the language of flowers is that it works equally well for a single flower stem, a small bunch of flowers, a bountiful bouquet, or a grand arrangement.

What should I do if I can't find a flower with the specific meaning I'm looking for?

The flower's meaning doesn't have to match the exact word you are thinking of, just the overall sentiment you want to express.

Why have I found a meaning for a flower that is different from what is in this book?

At times, in other sources, you may come across meanings other than the ones I have given. This is because the language of flowers has been used for thousands of years and across all cultures, leading to multiple meanings for many flowers. To keep *A Bouquet of Words* to a manageable size, I chose only one or two meanings for each flower. If you find a new meaning that resonates with you, I suggest making note of it (there are plenty of spaces in the book where you can do this).

To note, all the meanings I chose are based on historical information; I just limited the number I included.

The flower I want to use has two meanings; do I need to use both of them?

No. Pick the meaning that works for your message. You do not need to use both meanings at the same time.

Why do some varieties of flowers have meanings for each colour they come in, and some don't?

Even though many flowers come in more than one colour, only some of them specify a meaning for each of those colours. For example—chrysanthemums come in white, red, orange, yellow, pink, burgundy, cream, purple, and green, yet they only have a general meaning (cheerfulness). While tulips have an overall meaning (perfect love), every colour also has its own meaning (pink/caring, purple/elegance, orange/enthusiasm, red/true love, white/forgiveness, and yellow/there is sunshine in your smile).

I found some flowers having meanings for each colour they come in and some not, to be consistent in all of my research.

Should I use just one flower to convey my message or can I use many?

This is totally up to you. To portray an emotion or message you can keep things simple by choosing one flower to represent your sentiment, or get creative and choose many to create layers of meaning.

What should I do if a flower I want to use isn't available?

If a flower is not available to you, look for other ways to include it. See the bonus list **No Fresh Flowers—No Problem**.

Spelling

If you're used to American English you may think I have lots of spelling errors in my book, things like 'colour' instead of 'color' and 'recognise' instead of 'recognize'. The fact is, I am a dual citizen of Canada and the UK, and write using British English. It may seem odd to you at first, but hopefully you'll soon get used to it and find it charming in its own way.

ABOUT ME

Up until now I have had two rewarding careers, one as an early childhood educator and one as a florist.

I loved being a teacher. The children were inquisitive, creative, thoughtful, active, and always keen to learn. Each day differed from the one before, and there was always a new adventure to conquer.

When my teaching days came to an end, I knew exactly what I wanted to do—I wanted to become a florist.

I began training in my hometown of Vancouver, Canada. Then, over the years, I went on to continue my learning in London, Dublin, North Carolina, Portland, and Seattle. When I felt I was ready, I started my own floral business. Weddings, funerals, weekly deliveries and special orders were all part of the work week.

But my favourite thing about my work as a florist was hosting workshops. Workshops incorporated my enthusiasm for teaching with my knowledge of flowers.

Writing *A Bouquet of Words* has allowed me the opportunity to do that in another way. I hope you enjoy what I have to share with you.

Mary x

www.marykelava.com | Mary@marykelava.com
www.facebook.com/mary.kelava
www.instagram.com/marykelava

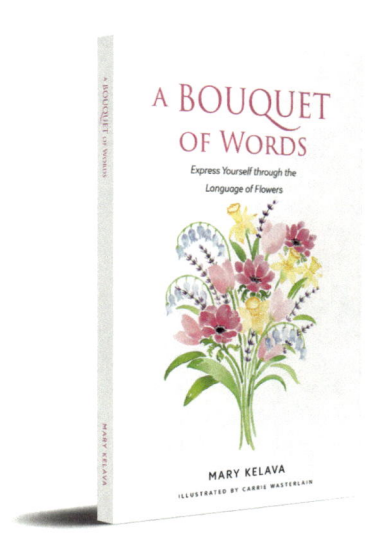

LEAVE A REVIEW

For a self-published author like myself, reviews mean the world! Please leave an honest review—yes, even critques—on the platform from which you purchased the book. I read every one!

Thank you.